Contents

Introduction

Welcome to the *Play Banjo Today! Songbook*. This book is for players who have worked their way through *Play Banjo Today! Level 2*. The material presented is an extension of the styles and techniques in the *Level 2* book and includes chord-melody arrangements, melodic-style Celtic tunes, and a special inside look at the wonderful techniques of the late John Hartford. Mr. Hartford was one of the most original and innovative players to ever pick the banjo. Two of his outstanding techniques are found throughout this book; both are an extension of the left hand bluegrass techniques you are already familiar with. The *double pull-offs* and *hammer-ons* (found in "Cripple Creek") enable the player to perform at extremely fast tempos (without picking fast)—a sure way to add excitement and variety to your repertoire! The second technique involves the use of *chromatic* chord shapes to embellish a melody ("Sweet Sunny South—high break" and "Lorena"). Chromatic means a series of notes is played, ascending or descending, a half step apart. An easy way to play chromatic runs on the banjo would be to play the notes on every fret along one string. On the piano you would play a scale starting on any note using every key. When playing the arrangements, keep the melody front and center. To do this, it's important to *know the melody* to at least one verse and chorus. I'd suggest singing the pieces with the arrangements as written, as well as using the backup techniques found in *Level 2*. If you don't wish to sing it's even more important to have the words and melody in your mind as you play. When you maintain this point of focus the melody will find its place naturally. It will also help you play in smooth, even time. Happy pickin'!

About the Author

Colin O'Brien is a nationally-touring performer based in Nashville, Tennessee. He plays guitar, fiddle, dances foot percussion and yes, he plays banjo. When not entertaining on the road, O'Brien may be found dancing in his front yard on the banks of the Cumberland River with his fiddle and banjo as the General Jackson steamboat rounds Hartford's Bend. He invites you to say hello at www.colingobrien.com

The Ultimate Self-Teaching Method! Songbook

Play Banjo Today! Songbook

Featuring 10 Folk & Traditional Favorites!

PLAYBACK+
Speed • Pitch • Balance • Loop

To access audio visit:
www.halleonard.com/mylibrary
Enter Code
3212-6106-6002-4444

Arranged and recorded by Colin O'Brien

ISBN 978-1-4803-2166-3

HAL•LEONARD®
CORPORATION
7777 W. BLUEMOUND RD. P.O. BOX 13819 MILWAUKEE, WI 53213

In Australia Contact:
Hal Leonard Australia Pty. Ltd.
4 Lentara Court
Cheltenham, Victoria, 3192 Australia
Email: ausadmin@halleonard.com.au

Visit Hal Leonard Online at
www.halleonard.com

Song Structure

Most songs have different sections that might be recognizable by any or all of the following:

- **Introduction** (or "Intro"): This is a short section at the beginning that "introduces" the song to the listeners.

- **Verses**: One of the main sections of the song—the part that includes most of the storyline—is the *verse*. There will usually be several verses, all with the same music but each with different lyrics.

- **Chorus**: Perhaps the most memorable section of the song is the *chorus*. Again, there might be several choruses, but each chorus will often have the same lyrics and music.

- **Bridge**: This section makes a transition from one part of a song to the next. For example, you may find a bridge between the chorus and next verse.

- **Outro**: Similar to the "intro," this section brings the song to an end.

Fermata ⌢

This symbol tells you to hold the note(s) longer than the normal time value. You will often see a fermata at the end of a song over the final note or chord.

Repeats & Endings

Repeat signs ‖: :‖ tell you to repeat everything in between them. If only one sign appears :‖ , repeat from the beginning of the piece.

First and Second Endings

Play the song through the first ending, repeat back to the first repeat sign, or beginning of the song (whichever is the case). Play through the song again, but skip the first ending and play the second ending.

D.S. al Coda

When you see these words, go back and repeat from this symbol: 𝄋

Play until you see the words "To Coda," then skip to the Coda, indicated by this symbol: ⊕

Now just finish the song.

Cripple Creek

American Fiddle Tune

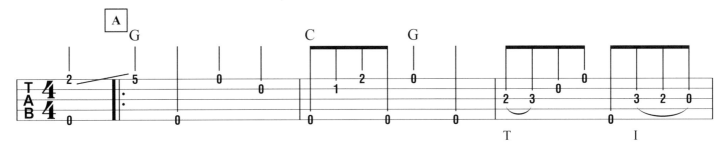

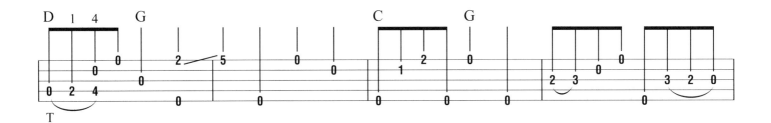

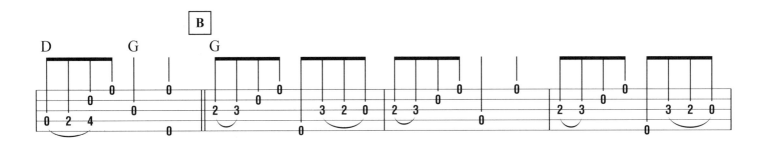

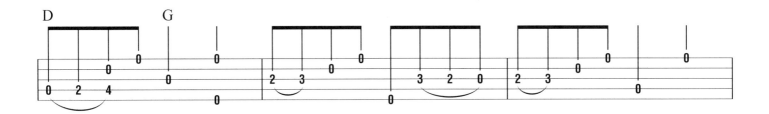

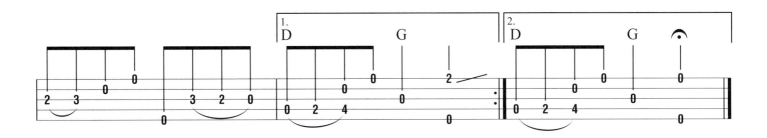

Drowsy Maggie

Traditional Irish

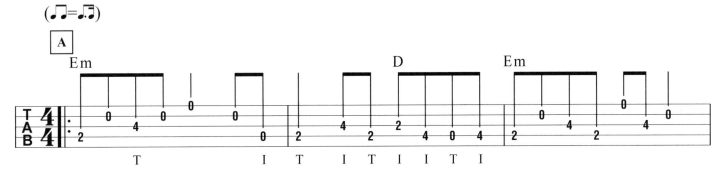

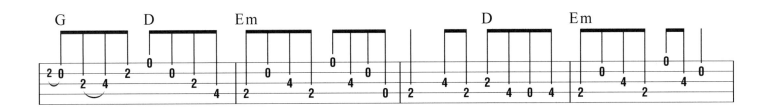

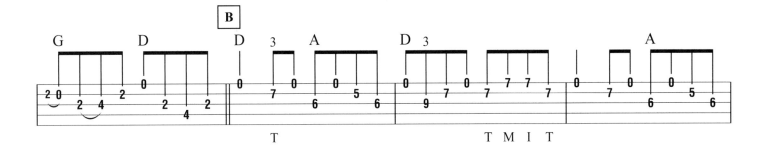

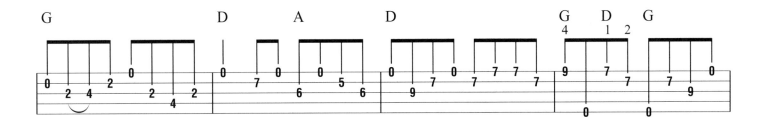

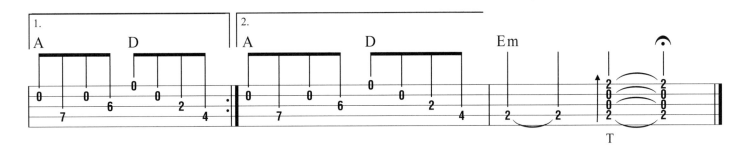

Greensleeves

Sixteenth Century Traditional English

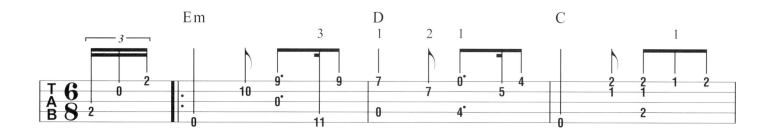

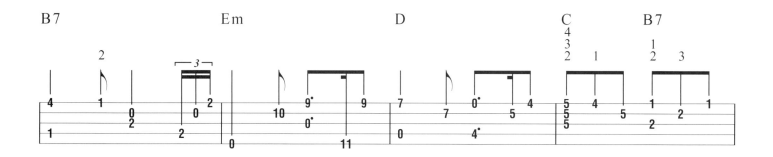

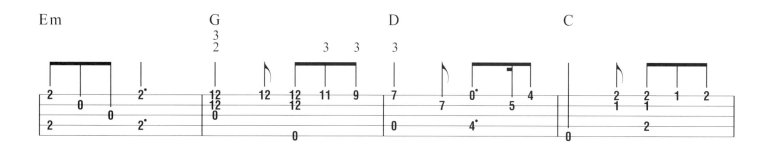

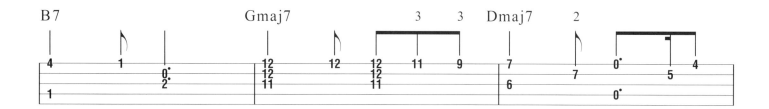

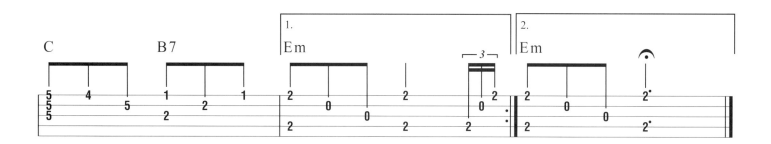

8

Harvest Home

Traditional Irish

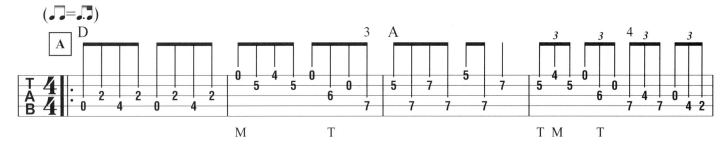

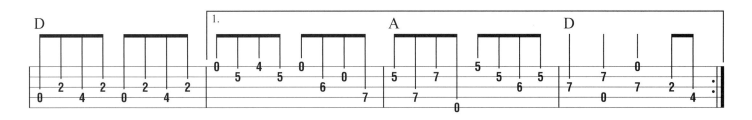

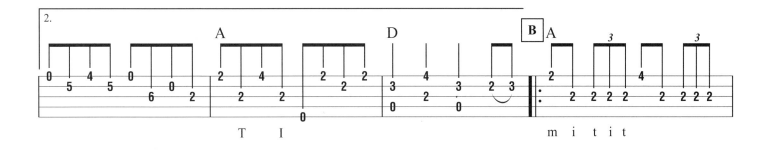

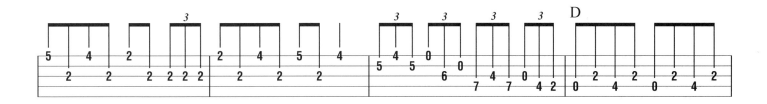

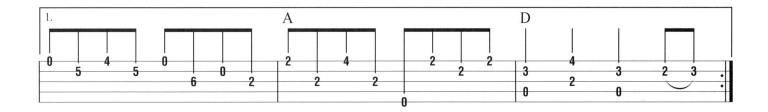

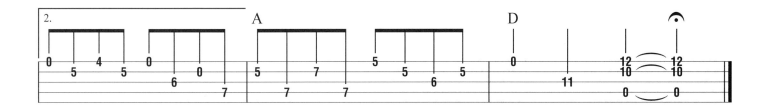

Jesu, Joy of Man's Desiring

Johann Sebastian Bach

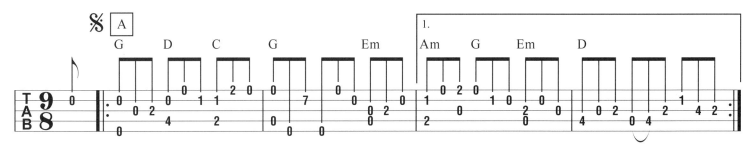

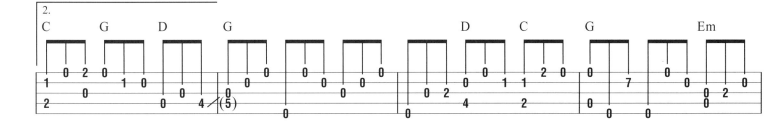

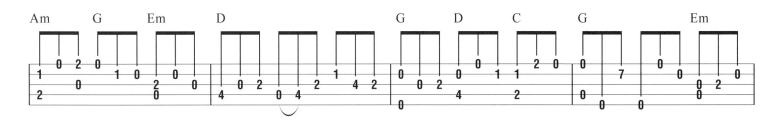

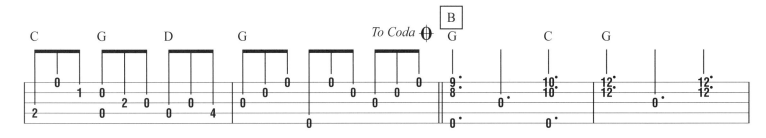

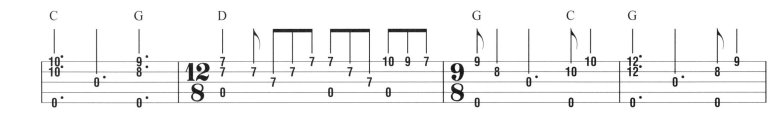

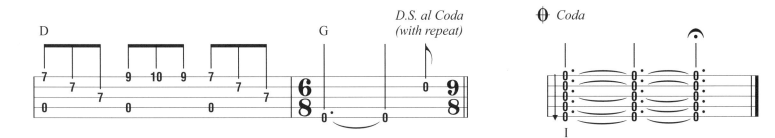

Lorena

Traditional

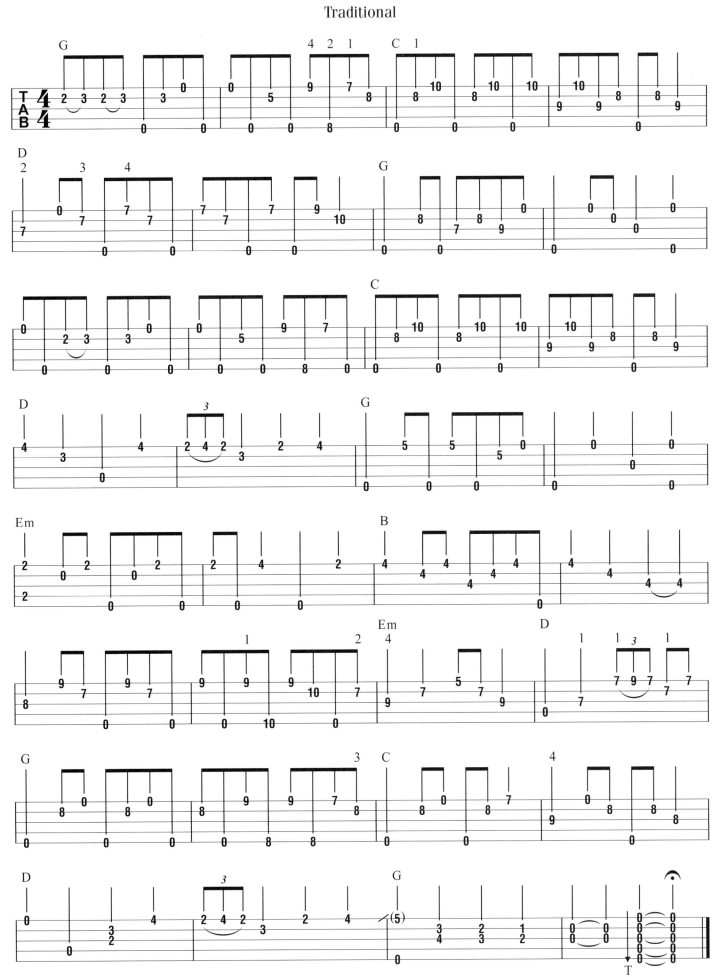

The Morning Star

Traditional Irish

Swing (♪♪=♪.♪)

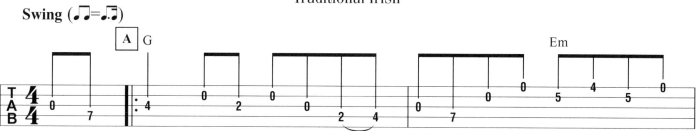

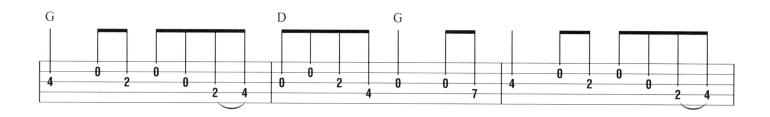

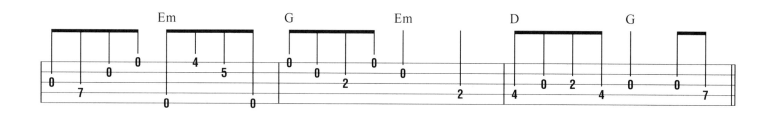

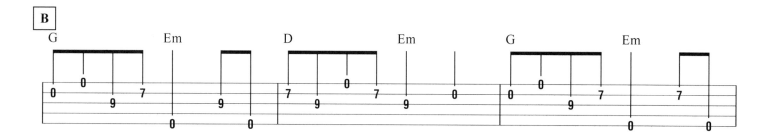

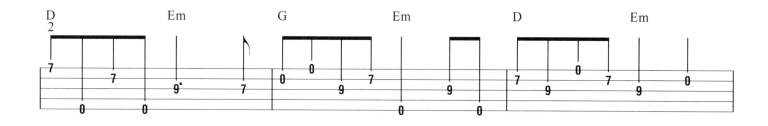

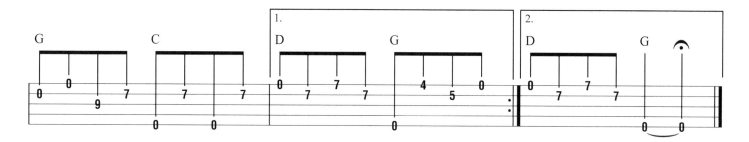

The Star Spangled Banner

Words by Francis Scott Key
Music by John Stafford Smith

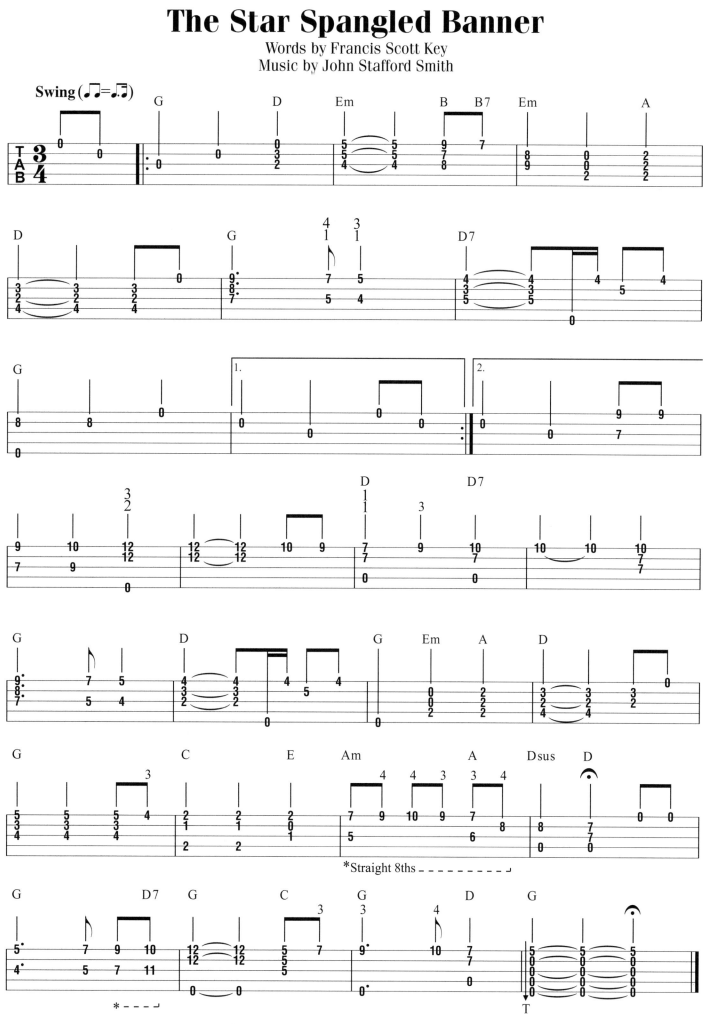

Stone's Rag

Traditional

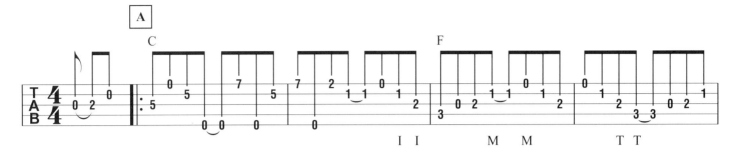

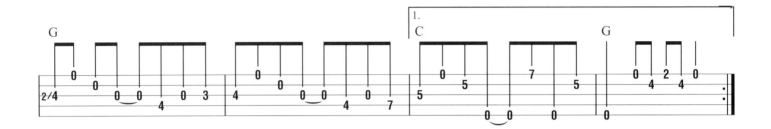

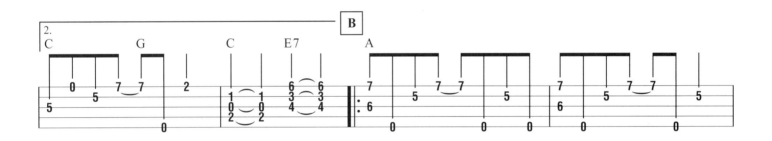

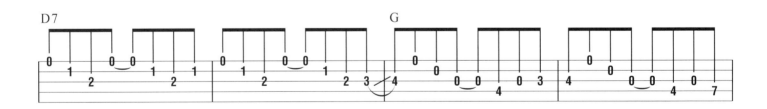

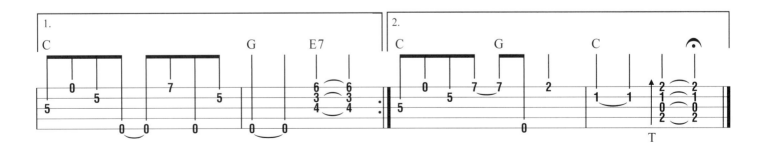

Sweet Sunny South

Traditional

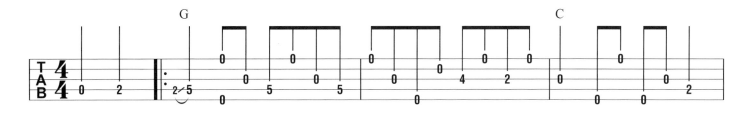

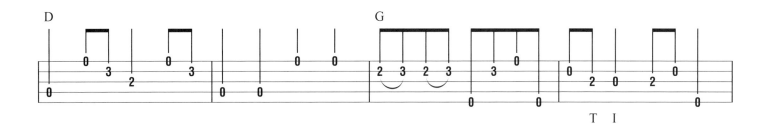

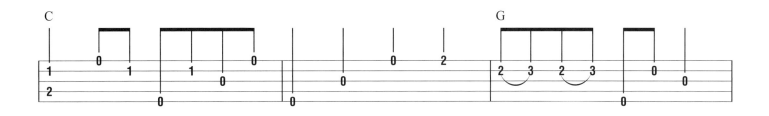

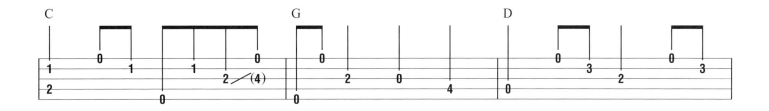

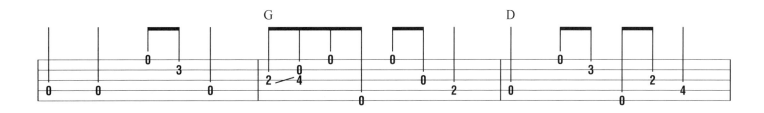

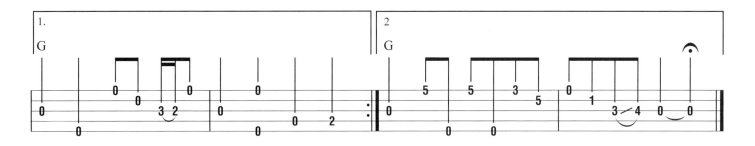

Sweet Sunny South–High Break

Traditional

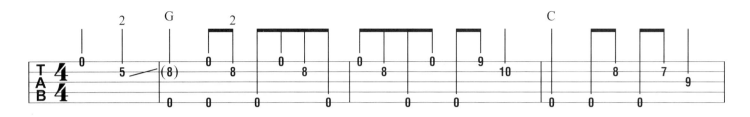

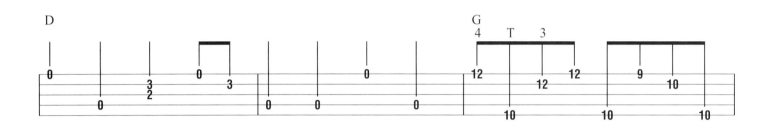

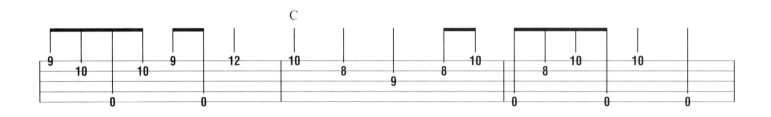

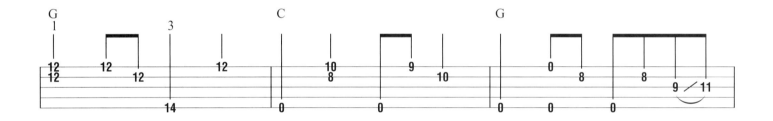

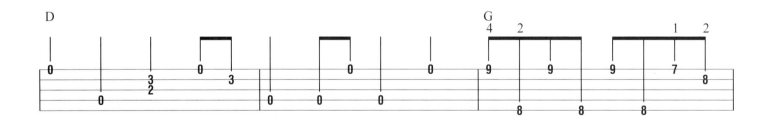

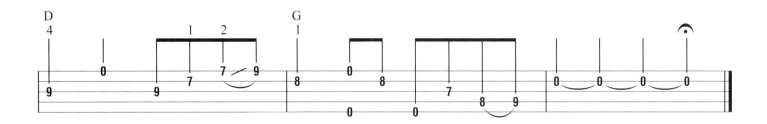